White Village

White Village

Poems in Classical Chinese

Yi Byŏng-ho

A Dual-Language Edition
With Parallel Texts

Translated by
Sung-Il Lee

RESOURCE *Publications* · Eugene, Oregon

WHITE VILLAGE
Poems in Classical Chinese

Resource Publications
An Imprint of Wipf and Stock Publishers
199 W. 8th Ave., Suite 3
Eugene, OR 97401

www.wipfandstock.com

PAPERBACK ISBN: 978-1-6667-7095-7
HARDCOVER ISBN: 978-1-6667-7096-4
EBOOK ISBN: 978-1-6667-7097-1

To the memory of
My revered grandfather,

白村 李炳浩

(1870–1943)

白村　李炳浩 (1870–1943)

九龍瀑

仙漱氣似清秋千尺長如立
不流玉井圓形通石底銀河倒勢
瀉雲欽書山雨戰光雞空白雷
喧響走收閃過九龍藏霹靂一湍
葱巃峽人共　白邦李炳浩

Holograph Manuscript of "The Waterfall of Nine Dragons"

Contents

Preface

The embryonic begetter of this book was the late Dr. Kim Jŏng-hwan, whose exploration and compilation of the poems of my grandfather, Yi Byŏng-ho, led to my publishing his collected writings in 2016. While carrying on research for his doctoral dissertation on the poetry of the students of "Mae-chŏn" Hwang Hyŏn, the renowned poet-scholar toward the end of the Chosŏn Dynasty, Mr. Kim Jŏng-hwan wrote a letter of inquiry to me in hopes of obtaining more research material on my grandfather, who was one of those belonging to the "School of Mae-chŏn."

At our first meeting, Mr. Kim Jŏng-hwan kindly handed me a set of the photo copies of my grandfather's poems and writings in prose he had collected. His handing it to me put me into a struggle to have my grandfather's poems and prose works published in a single volume. When I was in a state of bewilderment verging upon despair, torn between my ardent wish to have my grandfather's writings published in a volume and the realization that I am an ignoramus in classical Chinese, Professor Song Joon-ho, a senior professor of Yonsei University and a specialist of classical Chinese literature, extended help to me in preparing the typescript for a volume to contain my grandfather's poems and writings in prose.

After the publication of my grandfather's writings in their original texts, though confined to what Mr. Kim Jŏng-hwan has excavated, I have not been able to suppress my wish to have his poems reborn in English. I have been engrossed in translating Korean poetry into English in my zeal to introduce it to the world readership. Though fully aware of my being unprepared to undertake the work, I started translating my grandfather's poems into English, as it was unthinkable for me to let them fade away, unknown to the world.

My knowledge of classical Chinese is minimal. My case is comparable to that of a child who, having barely learned how to toy with a violin, tries to play Bach's *Partitas*! Yet I have persisted, burning with the wish to have my grandfather's lines heard in English, the language that has made me spend a major portion of my life, reading literature in it.

In the meantime, The Cultural Center of Kuryĕ (my grandfather's hometown) published a dual-language edition in 2019, utilizing the edition I published in 2016. In that bilingual edition, Mr. Shim Byŏng-tak, a scholar of classical Chinese, provided his

Korean translation running parallel with the original. While carrying on my English translation of the poems, I have consulted his Korean translation to make sure that my reading agrees with his. Though his reading does not always agree with mine, the bilingual edition has been a good reference in my coming to grips with the original lines of my grandfather's poems.

My long-deceased father, Professor Insoo Lee, would have made his father's poems come alive in English verse much superior to mine. His untimely death bereft him of that privilege, bequeathing his unfulfilled task on me as paternal legacy. I present my translation of my grandfather's poems, hoping that my overstepping the boundary of my literary achievement will be condoned by the readers.

Sung-Il Lee
January, 2023

Acknowledgments

I thank Mr. Stanley H. Barkan, Publisher and Editor of Cross-Cultural Communications, Professor Robert E. Bjork, of Arizona State University, Professor John M. Hill, formerly of The United States Naval Academy, and Dr. Danna R. Messer, of ARC Humanities Press, who complied with my request to write comments endorsing this book of mine. Special thanks are due to Mr. Barkan, who carefully went through my manuscript in his ardor to see my book published with the least shortcomings. I also thank Professor Kyung Hwan Moon, a former colleague of mine at Yonsei University, for his insightful comments, which made me reread my lines with the eyes of a reader detached from personal absorption. (SL)

Introductory Note on the Poet

Yi Byŏng-ho (李炳浩, 1870–1943), pen-named Paek-chon (白邨), was born in Kuryĕ, Chŏlla Province, Korea, in a family with scholarly heritage. Having been initiated into classical Chinese studies by his father early in his childhood, he later became a student of the renowned poet-scholar, Hwang Hyŏn (黃玹, 1855–1910), pen-named Mae-chŏn (梅泉), and, later, came to be reputed as one of the noted members of the "School of Mae-chŏn" ("梅泉詩派") that inherited the literary spirit and scholarship of Hwang Hyŏn. Hwang Hyŏn committed suicide in despair upon the country's losing her national sovereignty in 1910. After the demise of Hwang Hyŏn, his students compiled and published the collected writings of their mentor, "Mae-chŏn-jip" ("梅泉集"), in August, 1911. Yi Byŏng-ho was one of the five key members, who initiated and fulfilled the project, along with Wang Su-hwan (王粹煥), Pak Chang-hyŏn (朴暢鉉), Yoon Jong-gyun (尹鍾均), and Kwŏn Bong-su (權鳳洙), the foremost students of Hwang Hyŏn.

Born toward the closure of the Chosŏn (朝鮮) Dynasty, and living through the dark years till the country regained her national sovereignty in 1945, two years after his death, Yi Byŏng-ho had to suffer from the discrepancy between the vision of life he harbored and what he had to face in reality. The only way allowed for him to find any compromise between the stark realities and the dream and the ideal he harbored as a poet was to compose lines that depict the disparity between the dream-world and the realities. Many of his poems are about the sublimity and grandeur of nature as revealed to the eyes of people living in the world of dust. The reader, however, should not read these lines as instances of *contemptus mundi*. They should rather be read as depiction of the dream-world he envisioned, while living a life in misery—poverty and spiritual torpor. Here is a poem his friend Hwang Wŏn (黃瑗)—his mentor Hwang Hyŏn's younger brother—wrote to celebrate his sixtieth birthday:

> Your graceful face makes all onlookers enamored of you,
> And your kind and tender heart instills delight in them.
> Born in a scholars' family, you have grown old in poverty;
> Yet, endowed with serene temper, you ever remain peaceful.

Your poetic spirit lies in between Bai Jui's[1] and Lu You's;[2]
And when you are inspired, you even excel them in sublimity.
You walk with poise and calm, and your voice is clear and warm;
As you recite your lines, they ring like jade rolling on the petals.
You enjoy composing verses, with a ruddy face and white hair;
Under the autumn sky, a crane's song echoes the tune on a lyre.
As you chat, holding a wine-cup, near the chrysanthemums,
Wind-blown haze crystallizes to dewdrops rolling down petals. (My translation)

君貌妍華人皆愛
君性寬雅人皆悅
生於儒家老於貧
性不戚戚能安逸
詩在香山放翁間
往往得意清商發
步驟平穩響瀏亮
珠翠嫣然花間出
紅顔白髮善唫詩
鶴唳秋空和錦瑟
把酒笑談菊花傍
風流靄如花露結 (黃瑗, "壽李白邨")

The eulogy Hwang Wŏn bestowed on his friend Yi Byŏng-ho as man and poet
manifests itself in a poem the latter composed when a senior friend of his, Yi Chŏng-jik
(李定稷), pen-named 'Sŏk-jŏng'(石亭), visited him at Ku-ryĕ in 1942:

Though mounts loom to block you, you've sought this village;
In this early spring, snowy wind has not yet completely gone.
In dim lamplight your old brush glides, bearing cloud and fog;
Though your body wanes, you still hear the crane in the wind.
My hut is shabby, but I am delighted that you stay overnight;
Grown old, you are glad to see a man smacking of some gift.

---

[1] Bai Juyi (香山 白居易, 772–846 A.D.) was a renowned poet of the Tang (唐) Dynasty China.
[2] Lu You (陸游, 1125–1209 A.D.) was a historian and poet of the Southern Song (南宋) Dynasty China.

18

Deep into night we don't feel tired of chatting and laughing,
Till we realize, all of a sudden, that the moon fades at dawn. (My translation)

海岳迢迢訪碧城
早春風雪未全晴
紅燈筆老雲霞氣
病枕天寒鸛鶴聲
貧屋正勤留客意
暮年猶切愛才情
夜深談笑還忘倦
已見龍岡曉月生 ("與石亭拈劉隨洲集得城字")

Reunion of two friends, who share love for poesy and spiritual kinship, is described here without any exaggeration of its joy, and what overflows is the warmth of friendship between two men, who delight in their reunion at the small hut of the poet.

The major achievements of Yi Byŏng-ho are to be sought in his vigorous effort to create poetic societies in order to perpetuate the poetic spirit of his mentor Hwang Hyŏn. After the demise of Hwang Hyŏn, Yi Byŏng-ho, in his ardor to inherit and perpetuate his mentor's poetic spirit, created a number of poetic societies, such as "The Poetic Society of the Dragon Lake Bower" ("龍湖亭詩契"), founded in 1917, "The Poetic Society of Pong-sŏng" ("鳳城詩社"), founded in 1924, "The Poetic Society of Orchid and Bamboo" ("蘭竹社"), founded in 1929, "The Poetic Society of Kon-yang" ("壺陽吟社"), founded in 1933, and "The Poetic Society of Pang-jang" ("方丈詩社"), founded in 1936. In all of these poetic societies, he assumed the role of a key member, and vigorously participated in and led their literary activities.

All these poetic societies were created and maintained in the spirit of inheriting and preserving the cultural legacy the men of letters wished to revitalize at a time when the whole nation was suffering from spiritual torpor and pessimism after the loss of national sovereignty in 1910. Yi Byŏng-ho edited and published two anthologies containing the poems composed and recited at the poetic gatherings: *The Poetry of Mount Chiri* ("智異山詩集"), published in 1936, and *The Poetry of Pong-sŏng* ("鳳城詩稿"), published in 1937. (SL)

19

Poems

At the Gravesite of "The Crown Prince in Hempen Wear"[1]

The crown prince's soul has been hovering for a thousand years,
While a lone deserted mound drifts in the empty mountain.
Pitiful are the trees standing in a row before the Dragon-Horse Hill;
Every single leaf remains green, bearing their unchanging loyalty.

麻衣太子陵

磊落千秋太子靈
空山一墓獨飄零
可憐龍馬臺前樹
尚帶忠魂葉葉青

---

[1] The son of King Kyŏng-sun (敬順王, on the throne 927–935), the last monarch of the Unified Shilla, left the royal palace upon the downfall of the kingdom, to become a wanderer, preferring to live in anonymity, and died in obscurity. People called him '麻衣太子'('The Crown Prince in Hempen Wear').

Chang-an Temple of Mount Kŭm-gang

The unearthly scenery of hermits' world unfolds here;
Dark stream flows on, circling white rocks, tumbling.
The world-embracing light of Buddha shines in this sight;
Who will recall the glory and shame of the dusty world?
The sky pours down on the cliff a thousand-foot snowfall,
And the clear stream washes away the deep layer of dust.
As I bid a reluctant farewell to leave, heading for the south,
April flowers bloom on every tree exuberant in spring.

金剛山長安寺

蓬瀛面目十分眞
白石蒼流曲曲新
普德光明如此境
衆生榮辱竟何人
天垂絶壁千尋雪
地洗清溪萬古塵
寒暄迴與南中別
四月繁花樹樹春

The Waterfall of Nine Dragons

The chilly air of the waterfall makes it feel like autumn;
A thousand-foot tall rainbow shoots up, not to be shaken.
The deep pool is crystal-clear, swirling on the rocky floor;
The Milky Way turns over to pour down upon the clouds.
The blue mountain trembles in foggy rain hiding its color;
In bright sunrays, a deafening thunder resounds endlessly.
I have heard that nine dragons dwell in that deep cave;
The abysmal dark of the pool makes an onlooker shudder.

九龍瀑

仙仙灝氣似清秋
千尺長虹立不流
玉井圓形通石底
銀河倒勢瀉雲頭
青山雨戰光難定
白日雷喧響未收
聞道九龍藏窟宅
一淵蒼黝使人愁

The Valley of Ten-Thousand Waterfalls[1]

Ten-thousand waterfalls pour into pools reflecting the blue sky;

How many years ago did the four hermits roam here together?

The royal bird sings under the moon, while a flute tune flows on;

A dragon spews out thick clouds, causing the downpour of rain.

Thanks to rare fortune, I happened to be away from the dusty world;

I have fulfilled a wish for the next world's life far ahead of others.

I wish to tell those who left their names for posterity to remember:

You, who vied to leave beautiful lines behind, all of you, did so in vain.

萬瀑洞

瀑瀑成潭漾碧天

四仙遺蹟問何年

鸞聲逗月篁笙遠

龍氣噓雲白雨懸

曠世奇緣遊物外

此生餘恨在人前

寄言今古題名客

爭及諸家麗句傳

---

[1] "The Valley of Ten-Thousand Waterfalls" (萬瀑洞) is a ravine in Mount Kŭm-gang, where there are a
great number of waterfalls.

Visiting Pak the Mountain Man at Maga Hill

As rocks stood like gate poles, I didn't have to knock at a door to enter;
On seeing each other, the mountain man and I immediately became friends.
From a clear fountain crystalline dewdrops roll down to soak the sand;
Like a flower shivering in the cold, the moon is hung on a jade-like branch.
Among the clouds in the tranquil night, a cave is there for him to dwell in;
On the border of the sky is perched a crane's nest a man took for residence.
Having sought an unearthly place, I have become another who strolls in it;
Do not laugh at me for having come here, wearing the dust of man's world.

摩訶衍同朴晴崗

巖扃高關不煩敲
一見崗公卽結交
泉潔丹砂鳴玉溜
花寒明月上瓊梢
雲間夜靜金鰲窟
天畔人來碧鵑巢
尋眞我亦逍遙客
莫將塵累謾相嘲

On the Piro Peak[1]

As I turn to east from Piro Peak, the sea stretches endlessly.
The earth remains immobile; where, then, does it have links?
Soaring high for countless ages far above the dusty world,
A thousand peaks, bowing humbly, pay homage to the sky.
Though in the shape of Buddha, they are only rocks, after all;
Till my eyes reach their bound, fog spreads to block my view.
I laugh at my small self shrunk to turn into a mustard seed;
I sigh in the howling wind, while all my thoughts disappear.

毘盧峰

毘盧東望海無邊
大陸不動何處連
萬古崔嵬迷下界
千峰揖謙拱諸天
形同彌勒終爲石
地極扶桑但是烟
自笑此身爲芥子
長風太息意茫然

---

[1] Piro Peak is the highest of the peaks of Mount Kŭm-gang.

The Rocky Columns Standing on the East Sea[1]

The spirit of Mount Kŭm-gang raised these rocky columns on the sea;
Standing like pillars of jade pushed out of water, they brighten the sea.
While the sun is shining bright, the rising foams throng to dash ashore;
As the night deepens, the roar of the waves becomes louder in the dark.
The waves keep rushing and dashing ashore only to collapse and yield;
Though a picture may be drawn, or a poem composed, neither will do.
I would rather wield my brush in a big swish on a moonlit panel
To leave an immortal name for this bower that will live on forever.

通川叢石亭

金剛祖脈海隅成
玉立叢叢洞府明
日煖泡漚堆作勢
夜深波濤激爲聲
一顚一拜終緣癖
宜畫宜詩未盡情
大筆楣頭如曙月
關東特出此亭名

---

[1] "The Rocky Columns"(叢石亭) are the rocky formations on the east coast of Korea. They rise above the sea level, as if they were being pushed up from under the sea.

Mount Kŭm-gang on the Sea

Heaven has raised Mount Kŭm-gang both on land and sea;
Sea and mountain share one spirit, unseen by the world.
While shadows of rising and sinking rocks linger on the sails,
The mirror-like sea reflects their many shapes and poses.
Night chill threatens snow and frost with the rising mist;
The moon brightens, shining on the cranes flying in the clouds.
Now mirage and winding mist have fully revealed themselves,
The unfathomable skill of the Creator must've reached its limit.

海金剛

天作金剛西復東
海山氣脈暗相通
浮沈幻影搖帆上
碨礌成形落鏡中
夜冷雪霜蒸水府
月明鸞鶴翥雲空
蜃樓蝸殼爲眞面
媧石神功鍊已窮

At a Gathering at Dragon Hall

(A gathering of seventeen men of letters)

Since olden days this region has taken pride in producing poets;

And they have gotten together in this hall year after year.

The wide-open field provides a thoroughfare for the swallows;

In the thin rain falling on the river, white gulls wave their wings.

To welcome the fair season when flowers bloom to adorn the field,

We lift bowls to cheer one another, as we take turns to read our lines.

Can we not compare the gathering of ours today in this hall

To the feast the ancient poets held at "The Orchid Bower"?[1]

會于龍臺

(會者十七人)

此鄉從古韻人多

歲歲龍臺每一過

兩岸平蕪玄鳥路

半江疎雨白鷗波

堃花初發酬佳節

樽酒相尋放浩歌

借問名區今日會

蘭亭舊事較如何

---

[1] "The Orchid Bower" is literal translation of "蘭亭," an ancient pavilion in China, where men of letters are known to have gotten together to hold a banquet, in which they recited the poems they composed.

While Chatting at Night in Sado Village[1]

Surrounded by moist bamboos stands a cottage with clean air;
Visitors awake from their dreams in the chill of the frosty moon.
The mountain thick with trees echoes the sound of beating cloth;
While we drink warmed wine in dim light, the wild pheasants coo.
Promising to get together again when chrysanthemums bloom,
We bid farewell to one another, reconfirming friendship at old age.
As love for old friends can never fade, no matter how fast time flies,
Some rush to town to buy more wine, though it is deep into night.

沙圖夜話

四隣水竹一堂清
霜月微寒客夢驚
紅樹山深村杵動
青燈酒暖野鷄鳴
相尋不負黃花約
久別偏憐白髮情
爲愛故人勤志在
夜深沽酒向江城

---

[1] 'Sado' is the name of a village in Kuryĕ, the poet's birthplace.

Sending off Friends at Isan Bower

Autumn light thickens, as we drift down the river on a boat;
In the endless west wind, the shadow of wild geese flows on.
Now the wine crock is empty, you are also leaving at dusk;
Watching the clouds float over red leaves, I lean on the bower.

二山樓　送同社諸益

五峯秋色上江舟
無數西風鴈影流
酒盡斜陽君且去
白雲紅葉獨凭樓

Humming at Night at Isan Bower

As wind blows on the withering lotus leaves, water birds fly off;
The lane meanders through the pines, dimly lit by the moon.
In the garden famed for good stones, men have already grown old;
When streams and hills fill the earth, where are you bound, travelers?
Wine sent from the village there makes the season more delectable;
But when a loiterer ascends the bower, dusk falls unfailingly.
Deep into the night I struggle to compose a poem I have promised;
I bring it to my friend, unaware of my clothes getting wet with dew.

二山樓　夜吟

老荷風動水禽飛
一路松凉月影微
花石名園人已老
溪山滿地客何歸
前村送酒成佳節
遊子登樓又落暉
半夜催詩難負約
行尋不覺露沾衣

Sitting in my Room ("Moored Boat") till Dawn

Frosty air blows on the candle lit in a mountain abode;
Cockcrow is heard, coming through the bamboo grove.
A solitary sojourner keeps humming lines for his lone self;
Though the moon is about to fade, he cannot fall asleep.

岸船室 曉坐

霜氣吹山燭
雞聲生澗竹
幽人獨自吟
月落猶未宿

A Small Gathering on the Winter Solstice Night

Through the bamboo grove turning white a moss-laden lane winds;
Old friends are happy to see one another's wrinkled face and white hair.
While reciting newly-composed lines under a cold-defying apricot tree,
Self-summoned guests drink tart wine near a stream flowing cold.
Fishing and collecting wood in the right season, we follow old custom;
And even in poverty-ridden winter, people get married for posterity.
Hunger-stricken families are not afraid of an impending war;
Their only wish is to see the world going on with good harvest.

冬至夜 小會

白竹蒼苔一路通
故人顏髮喜相同
新詩速客寒梅下
濁酒招隣碧澗東
季世漁樵追古宅
窮冬嫁娶見淳風
貧家不患干戈動
祇願生平歲歲豐

Getting Together Again with Sŏpa at Uchŏn Hall

We bad farewell in the morn before the window dimming now in the dusk;
As the year's end nears, my heart darkens to recall what has gone wrong.
Slender bamboos line up like a fence to surround a tidy study lounge,
While over the nearby mountain cold clouds thicken, threatening rain.
What's the use of amassing literary knowledge when one has grown old?
In this turbulent time my wish to live plowing the field looks unlikely;
You spend your old age, taking care of a few paddies, in this rural area;
I cannot but envy you for leading an untainted life that suits a scholar.

與西坡復會愚川室

朝窓惜別到斜暉
歲暮悲懷事事違
細竹連籬書榻淨
斷山催雨凍雲飛
壯年文字功何在
叔世農桑計又非
五畝田園堪送老
羨君清致一儒衣

More Lines Composed on the Same Night

As night deepens, wine-crocks are called for even more frequently;
Though we wear white hair, how can't we be elated in this bright room?
Mountain shadow is cast over this secluded village with mulberry fields;
As apricots bloom near the cozy hut, the sound of rain becomes louder.
Wandering about for ten years was for the pleasure of drifting on a boat;
When will the whole clan get together in a hut hidden behind a bush?
When can I find my kindred souls in a friendly neighborhood, where
I exchange lines with them, visiting one another, morning and evening?

是夜復賦

夜闌西舍酒頻過
白首青燈興若何
桑柘邨深山影近
梅花屋暖雨聲多
十年浪跡緣舟楫
幾日全家隱薜蘿
安得同隣三逕友
暮朝相逐放豪歌

Another Poem Composed on the Same Night

As I start grinding ink-stone under the dim lamplight,
The waning moon still dimly brightens the sky at dawn.
Cold-defying apricots bloom, enduring the night rain,
While the breath of spring blows, covering the mountain.

又

剔燈復開硯
缺月上曉空
寒梅一夜雨
春意滿山中

Yet Another Poem Composed on the Same Night

The sound of pounding crops already rings along the furrows;
The lanes leading to the village meander through the paddies.
Thanks to good harvest, news of wedding are heard more often;
In the year to come, paying taxes may become less burdensome.
Folks retaining high morale are happy to live under thatched roofs;
Though the county is small, it is surrounded by green mountains.
They gladly serve their precious chickens to treat their guests well.
Alas, while indulging in composing lines, I forgot to return home.

又

野渠鳴碓底
村路入田間
稔歲婚多就
新年稅漸閒
人高惟白屋
郡小盡青山
雞黍憐君意
沈唫却忘還

Yet Another Poem Composed on the Same Night

Letters can hardly arrive, crossing many a river and lake;
But having met again at this bower, we hug one another.
Now the sky has cleared up, we must be in a hurry to leave;
We only regret to see the setting sun loom before our horses.

又

江湖百里鴈書稀
芝塾相逢喜挽衣
即事天晴歸思急
馬首青山落日飛

Composed in a Rhyme Scheme Found in Mae-chŏn's Poetry

A dark stream flows on, while cold clouds float above, frowning;
I walk along the stream, lighting my way with a pine-knot torch.
On hearing the geese honk, a wayfarer thinks of his far-off home;
"My neighbors must be hastening to finish weaving before cockcrow."
Having no medicine to cure your illness, I sigh for my inability;
All I can do, bearing white hair, is to compose a poem to send to you.
Shapely rocks and lovely flowers remain the same while time passes;
The work inherited for generations is confined to a small piece of land.

次梅泉集中韻

一溪黝黑凍雲垂
松炬輝輝澗屐隨
遠客思家征鴈後
隣燈催織到鷄時
青囊無訣憐君病
白首成章送子詩
綺石名花依舊老
百年箕業小園池

Lamenting the Times

The village encroaches on the devastated farming field;
Yet for teaching the young, small schools are still built.
Alarmed to see the calendar showing the shifting of the years,
We hear the gong ringing, as if to announce jolly times ahead.
While pity wells in one's heart to see an old ailing friend suffer,
Books not yet read call the attention of one of meager learning.
A word of request I wish to give to one who judges hastily:
"When you hear me humming a poem, do not consider it vain."

又題五律嘆世

村犯荒田大
校因私塾成
曆驚雙臘改
鍾喜比時鳴
舊眼憐衰友
新書問小生
寄言輕薄子
休怪詠詩聲

Drinking with Friends by So-ah Stream

As sky has cleared up and bright weather is promised for afternoon,
We decide to wear usual outfit and get together near the stream.
Over the last ten years the pines on the sandy shore have grown old;
And they partake in our joy of composing lines over a crock of wine.
Hidden by the exuberant grass, the brown calves are barely seen;
As wind blows, the white gulls fly up to swarm in the clear sky.
The grass growing on the bank looks even greener after the rain;
Yearning and regrets lodged in our hearts will stay with us long.

會飲于所兒川邊

晴光嬾娜午陰流
巾屨相尋野水頭
十載沙田松已老
一樽詞賦客同遊
草深堤堰迷黃犢
風動汀洲起白鷗
兩崖江蘺經雨綠
古今情恨未應休

A Reply to the Poems of Yu-dang and Sŏk-jŏn

Having met you again in this world of a fairest scenery,
I am happier to hear the beautiful lines you've composed.
As I watch the petals drift in the rain falling on the mountain,
Clouds on that hill threaten the village blessed with many furrows.
The lamplight that lit our gathering gleams again as in a dream,
As I recall our hoary friend, who has drifted away on a lone boat.
Shall we be allowed to sit together again under a fair moon,
And sing aloud near a wine pot, jollily declaring we'll not part?

與西堂石田唱酬村塾

隔歲江湖始見君
琳琅詩話喜堪聞
一向花盡山中雨
百畝村深壘上雲
舊社青灯渾似夢
孤舟白髮獨離羣
安將明月同隣曲
尊酒行歌不暫分

Chatting with Paek-pa and a Few Other Friends at Night

The east wind blows on the trees to stir the soul of a wanderer;

Leaning on a staff, I follow a stream to arrive at a remote village.

Seats are ever ready to receive good old friends coming from afar;

His gate remains open, for he likes to watch the far-off mountains.

As the moon looms from clouds, many a village gets buried in quietude;

As the sound of rain comes through the bamboos, the lone window darkens.

Having wandered far and wide over the years, we are now finally together;

Now, let us indulge in the pleasure of exchanging lines over many a drink.

與白坡夜集小話

樹樹東風撼客魂

野笻隨水到荒村

爲迎好友常留榻

愛看名山不掩門

雲裡上燈千巷靜

竹間聽雨一窗昏

歷落江湖今見晚

喜將詩酒與相論

Lines Composed in Succession

Having built a hut above the white clouds,
I realize I have settled in a nest hard to reach.
Rugged rocks loom high, threatening with danger;
Old apricot trees lie fallen, buried in muddy clay.
One can at leisure easily attain poetic sentiments;
But as one tries to relive a spring dream, it only fades.
Holding a lantern, I open the window to look out;
I see many a tree casting its shadow under the moon.

又連賦五律

家住白雲上
認吾高處棲
岩頑危作渡
梅老倒粘泥
詩愁閒易得
春夢記還迷
回燈開牖見
午樹月陰低

Composed Extempore upon Meeting Yu-dang

I stroll to a neighboring village, stopping here and there;

People wrongfully tell me that my poetry has reached its zenith.

Where trees are low, a gate looks as tall as to reach a bird's nest;

When the field is immersed in water, a lane of swollen earth gives relief.

As I burn incense on a table, mountains renew their quietude;

The village is empty, for all are gone to the field to bring noontide meal.

Accompanying you, I wish to turn into a greedless loafer,

And lie in the shade of an apricot tree to indulge in daydreaming.

逢酉堂 連夜戲作

行盡村南與澗東

傍人錯道我詩窮

樹低門對禽巢上

水漲蹊生麥壟中

一榻焚香山更靜

四隣就餉午如空

携君仍作清狂客

醉臥梅陰夢放翁

At the First Gathering of a Few Friends at Pong-sŏng Bower

As the late sunbeams fall on slender bamboos and sparse pines,

I walk toward the bower to ascend it and share drink with friends.

In this remote village barley is ripening to brim over the field;

A far-off sailboat glides in the calm wind over the clear stream.

The altar built for praying for peaceful times remains a sad relic;

Young ones learn how to play the instruments for different music.

Though grown old, I wish to befriend those who will indulge with me,

Wearing straw hats for fishing, till we come to rest in an old castle.

第一回　鳳城樓小集

細竹疎松帶晚晴

登樓喚酒起余行

孤村麥熟山田厚

遠棹風恬野水明

盛世壇隍悲舊蹟

少年絲管學新聲

衰齡安得江湖伴

共買漁蓑臥古城

At the Fourth Gathering at Pong-sŏng Bower (I)

The blue beam of Royal-Bird Mountain fills the lone bower,
While the midday shade of the pines engirds the yard.
Far on the river, blown on by a fair breeze, a twin-sail boat drifts;
As the sun sets over a crumbling wall, green peaks soar in disarray.
A century-old monument for holding rituals remains only as a ruin,
To awakens us to the transience of glory in the rapid flow of time.
Watching the old custom being retained in the fair art of archery,
I hear the ringing of a gong and the beat of a drum pleasing my ears.

第四回　鳳城樓再會

鳳山蒼翠滿孤亭
卓午松陰遍戶庭
遠水風微雙帆白
荒城日落亂峰青
百年壇廟遺墟在
此地滄桑一夢醒
古俗重觀鄉射禮
一金一鼓喜堪聽

At the Fourth Gathering at Pong-sŏng Bower (II)

As cicadas' chirping grows faint to fade away,
The glow of the setting sun falls on old pines.
Heat persisting till late calls for a cold drink;
Exhausted with composing lines, we seek a cool shade.
A lane ends where a stream flows, separating the paddies;
Let the bower look on the peak soaring over the bamboos.
As we grow old, we cherish our gathering more and more;
Let us not neglect seeing one another in the days ahead.

第四回　鳳城樓再會 (續賦)

裊裊蟬聲遠

斜陽在古松

暑殷宜酒冽

吟苦就陰濃

路折田間水

樓依竹裏峰

晚因詩社重

休厭日相從

Lines Attached to the Collected Poems of Yong-jae

Remembering our studying together in the mountain wearing white clouds,
I count how many times chrysanthemums and orchids bloomed and wilted.
Though I try to recall your voice and face, I only hear silence and see void;
What remains are only the lines you left behind for those of us still alive.

Our county has seen real impersonation of the legend of a devoted wife:
Your life's companion you left behind deserves all the praise she receives.
Now we have printed your poems to make them live on for ages to come,
The eternally-bright moon will long shine on her room deep in her abode.

題慵齋詩集後

憶曾同榘白雲山
秋菊春蘭幾往還
怊悵音容空寂寞
但留詩句在人間

吾鄉復見舜欽妻
高氏令名較不低
能使棗梨長壽世
千秋明月映深閨

Lines Composed for Kam-ho Bower

Now we've rebuilt the bower with a few rafters on its old site,
The lake beam and the mountain color enter it, dazzling our eyes.
The wood that has grown old reaches the good neighborhood;
The scent lingering over the flowery stones makes one recall olden days.
Blown on by the soft breeze crossing the field, a white-sailed boat drifts;
Narrow lanes wind along entangled roots, and petals fall to dye streams.
When spring comes, some fishermen may happen to drop by here;
I fear they may tell the world outside what a paradise is hidden here.

次鑑湖亭

舊址重成屋數椽
湖光山色入蒼然
梓桑已老推仁里
花石留香感昔年
野渡風恬流白舫
雲根路細落紅泉
春來恐有漁郎到
洞裏桃源莫相傳

Lines Composed for Kam-ho Bower Again

A stroll leads me to an unearthly vale hidden by white clouds;
The meandering lane guides me to constantly changing scenery.
In mild weather thin rain falls to soak the early spring Memorial Day;
Passing by a poor village, I arrive where apricot flowers bloom.
At a lone bower I recall those who lived before in our country;
Having drifted into a mountain, I have become a guest from afar.
As I turn my eyes to east, green grass spreads on the waterside;
Close by the river stands a bower left by those who went ahead.

又鑑湖亭

白雲洞裏訪仙春
峽路風光面面新
暖日易成寒食雨
荒村隔在杏花隣
孤亭海內追先輩
一棹山中作遠賓
東望汀洲蘋藻綠
先生遺廟古江濱

On Entering the Precinct of Chŏn-ŭn Temple

A gush of rain on the rice flowers announces the new autumn;
Participants in our poetic gathering are all wearing white hair.
Where the trees' shadows and the mountain light cross in blue,
The temple gate remains shut, while a clear stream rushes on.

第七回　入泉隱寺途中

稻花一雨忽新秋
赴社遊人盡白頭
樹影山光交翠裏
寺門深隔碧溪流

Mourning for Master Pak Hyŏn-gok

While the years of his seventies were entrusted to rural life,
His love of poetry and graceful living ever deepened.
Enduring the pain of the turbulent years, he would hide tears;
And he would not waste his noble gift on worldly trifles.

Once stricken by illness, he found those few years slow-moving,
For medicine of marvel and divine elixir both proved powerless.
In the deep of the night, where does the crane's song come from?
Must be the hour when the moon sinks below Mount Pang-ho.

His old cottage where generations have lived overflows with warmth,
Being the home of brothers, who plow in the sun and read at night.
Walking ahead or following after, all the way to the burial ground,
The mourning kinsfolk move along the way clouds do.

The harvest of the field has been sent far, for poverty is no concern;
And his numerous offspring have already begun to show their gifts.
Pity to the flowers and the cottage with a thatched roof—
They can no more see the man, who loved them and liked to read.

My sojourn away from home through the season of snow and storm,
Alas, kept me from partaking in his funeral as one of the pole-bearers.
Now it is getting late in the year to mourn for his departed soul,
He in the nether world will surely forgive me busy in this world.

哭朴玄谷先生

七旬安養臥蓬蒿
詩禮風流老更豪
叔世滄桑堪掩涕
高才終未試牛刀

一病駸駸數歲遲
瓊漿玉液正無奇
夜深笙鶴知何處
正是方壺月墮時

古家邀福久氤氳
弟讀兄耕作一群
柩後柩前臨壙路
功緦宗黨侍如雲

千里齎糧不患貧
僉孫頭角已嶙峋
可憐花石茅溪屋
不見淳淳勸學人

窮冬風雪客他鄉
恨未攀輀到斧堂
一哭靈筵經歲晚
九原應恕我奔忙

Mourning for O Hyŏng-sun, Alias 'Twin Hills'

I recall the days when I followed you at Sang-sa Village;
Then we studied and played together like two brothers.
In front of the school where we read and whistled together,
Even now stand the same moonlit pines as in olden days.

Born kind-hearted, you were never allowed to stay alone;
Befriending hills and streams, you lived till you grew hoary.
Gray-haired brothers would sit before desks side by side;
The sight made me recall the four known to have lived in retreat.

One night, from the heavenly stream a bright star fell off;
Now in our county we shall find it hard to meet a wise man.
Though filial piety is declining, they don't follow the trend;
In performing funeral ceremony, they keep its old tradition.

Your elder brother left behind barely lives on in his nineties;
While mourning before your coffin, he faints as the sun sets.
Your lifelong companion now keeps her quiet abode alone;
Grief for your demise will reach far to the center of heaven.

挽吳雙山炯淳

憶曾追逐上沙村
同學同遊似弟昆
重翠軒前唫嘯地
至今松月典刑存

天賦溫溫德不孤
依然山澤告眉鬚
弟兄白髮聯床坐
如見千秋四皓圖

一夜江天隕少微
吾鄉自此哲人稀
孝衰不逐風潮變
殯葬猶從古禮歸

大耋奄奄伯氏存
柩前哭倒夕陽昏
百年相好今安在
此恨遙應徹九原

At a Temple on an Autumn Night

We each trod an unaccustomed road to get here for a gathering;
An evening for a noble game keeps us from the dusty world.
The starry stream in the autumn sky renders it unlike a night;
As clouds and trees deepen the mountain, we see only the sky.
From the quiet bower the gong rings, resounding to reach far,
While the talk of people exchanging cups is heard in lamplight.
Though we now well know the road running through the flowers,
How many years, I wonder, will pass till we read our lines again?

僧堂秋夜

初地相尋社事圓
清遊一夕絕塵烟
星河秋潔如無夜
雲木山深但見天
樓靜鍾音歸塔外
酒行人語在燈前
花間慣識曾行路
借榻看書問幾年

Upon Leaving a Temple

As the sun gracefully rises above the peaks,
Clouds flow on like a stream in the valley.
As a visitor takes off, inhaling the morning air,
Dew on the pine leaves drenches his clothes.

出寺口號

妍妍峰日出
潋潋洞雲歸
野客侵朝發
松滋濕滿衣

A Night at Ch'ŏn-ŭn Temple

As the moon comes out to fill the dewy sky,
Guests find it hard to sleep in a temple room.
A hundred rushes resound in the vale of peonies;
Wind at dawn blows over the paulownia leaves.
Though my lines may move the world, my body wanes;
Yet there will be time for the mountains to renew splendor.
Now we are granted poetic indulgence in a temple room,
Buddha will not frown at us while we spend a noisy night.

宿泉隱寺

滿空豐露月來時
塔廟雄深客睡遲
百道泉鳴紅藥院
五更風過碧梧枝
文章動世身偏老
山嶽增輝會有期
賴得禪房詩社重
我曹疎放佛應知

Upon Encountering Rain at Hwa-chŏn Temple

On the road to the famed mountain rugged stones are rare;
A cold stream flows, encircling a village, as if to embrace it.
New-sprung rice shoots wet with dew look soft and tender;
White herons afloat in the breeze fly on leisurely and slowly.
As drought goes on, scoops are busy to irrigate the paddies;
Densely arrayed trees provide a canopy that blocks sunrays.
Dressed for an excursion, I seek the fountain of miracle again,
To find the way to the emerald wall and the ruby well blocked.

華泉寺遇雨

路出名山惡石稀
冷冷一澗抱村歸
青秧露浥纖纖見
白鳥風恬滾滾飛
天旱桔槹爭細瀝
樹深襱襏避炎暉
巾鞋又訪靈源去
翠壁紅泉掩板扉

At Pong-sŏng Inn

Tall bamboos on the bank shake, chasing the birds away;
On the sprouting rice falls sparse rain, thin at noontide.
Green grass engirds the village till the river winds away;
And a lone fisherman's boat glides in the maze of rocks.
Youthful days are gone, as if a stream flows never to return;
What if we gulp down drink, can we detain time from fleeing?
What makes us happy at our reunion is exchanging our lines;
What need for lamenting wearing hemp[1] at this troubled time?

第八回　鳳城旅館唱酬

岸岸長竿打鳥飛

稻花疎雨午霖微

綠蕪村帶清江盡

白舫人穿亂嶂歸

短髮偏憐催逝水

芳樽那得駐斜暉

相逢寂喜詩緣重

叔世何須怨布衣

---

[1] "Wearing hemp" means not to take any position as a public official.

Composed at Pong-dong Hall at Night

As the Plow twinkles far away and the moon is about to fade,
In the chilly night wet with dew, a wayfarer cannot fall asleep.
Though none's here to play in answer to the tune of your pipe,
The stream and the high mountains will know by themselves.

鳳東軒夜題

星斗迢迢月落時
夜凉風露客眠遲
君簫一曲無人和
流水高山獨自知

Staying Overnight at Hwa-ŏm Temple

As the monk and the visitors sit together in a temple room,
White robe and black head-wear mingle in their shadows.
Deep at night welcome rain falls, beating the bamboos;
Those few lanterns in the quiet bower are dim in the clouds.
At a poetic gathering held in the mountain, who shall take charge?
As you command high fame in this land, we request you to do so.
Having gotten together at this sanctuary, let us not disperse soon:
When we step out into the busy world, we shall take separate roads.

宿華嚴寺

禪客追隨自一群
烏巾白衲影紛紛
夜深甘雨驟鳴竹
庵靜疎燈逈入雲
社事山中誰作主
詩名海內共推君
靈區且莫輕相別
門外滄桑路更分

At Yong-ho Bower with Chang-san Kim Sang-guk

Now spring is fading, thick green is spread over the mountain;
And the lone bower, as in olden days, stands in the pinewood.
As the howling wind beats the cliff, a dragon roars often;
As the sun heats up the sand, birds return on their own will.
Fragrant grass cannot lighten a sad wayfarer's heavy heart;
Yet holding a cup of wine, I can watch a dear friend's face.
You, who are drifting on a lone boat, holding a fishing rod,
I envy you for being so leisurely, sitting in the foggy rain.

第九回　同金倉山祥國登龍湖亭

卽事春殘綠遍山

孤亭依舊亂松間

長風打壁龍時吼

煖日烘沙鳥自還

芳艸難禁遊子恨

深樽更對故人顏

羨爾扁舟垂釣客

一江烟雨任他閒

At Ae-chŏn Dale

Light-footed with straw shoes on, I have arrived here in midday;
Mountain casts its shadow on the lane winding through the pines.
My friend is already crossing the river far over the reed bush;
The small tavern is still here near a willow tree drooping branches.
As the temple gets near, a gong rings to reach the floor of the stream;
As I finish composing a poem, sunset glow is cast on the wine-crock.
It was all in the past that a genuine poet lived; yet, though he's gone,
We, who wear white hair, have gotten together to renew his ardor.

第十回　艾川洞暢叙

野屐翩翩趁午天
峯陰松翠路微連
故人迥渡蒹葭水
小店自依楊柳烟
寺近寒鍾生澗底
詩成落日在樽邊
稽山已古風流遠
社事重成白髮年

At the First Meeting of Nan-juk (*"Orchid and Bamboo"*)

We chose a cool shade of pines to avoid inebriety in daylight;
Reclining in the shade of flowers, we invite a brief slumber.
Whenever we get together, we realize the rapid flow of time:
Sitting around a wine crock, we lament our hair turning white.

第一回　蘭竹社詩會

凉取松陰防午醉
暖依花影借安眠
相逢易感風光暮
共惜樽筵白髮年

At a Tavern near Chŏn-ŭn Temple

As leaves turn red and chrysanthemums bloom, it sure is late autumn;
In this fair season our promise has been fulfilled near the clear stream.
The village is deep-seated, and the color of the field is spread to the hill;
As the temple is near, the gong's ringing comes just across the river.
Surprised to see a man of renown, we hasten to receive him to our table;
We ascend the bower in the midst of the bamboos to open a wine crock.
As mountain shade darkens, fishermen and wood-cutters return home;
The glow of setting sun cast on the lane brings pathos to the wayfarers.

第二回 會于泉隱寺洞口酒樓

紅樹黃花政暮秋
佳辰此約儘清流
村深野色懸山麓
寺近鍾聲落水頭
倒屣忽驚名下士
開樽遲入竹間樓
峰陰漸黝漁樵下
一路斜陽動客愁

Following the Moon on My Way to Ji-chŏn-ri

Faint moon floats above the lone village;
And thin clouds veil the trees far away.
Walking on a dark road, I lean on my staff;
I try to stay on a lane winding along the ridge.

隨月訪芝川里 途中口號

微月澹孤村
薄雲迷遠樹
暝行但信筇
逼側田間道

Upon Ascending Yong-ho Bower

Clear and deep sound of springtime water becomes louder at noon;

A wayfarer worn and weary pushes the gate to ascend the bower.

Halfway on the rugged cliff stands a weather-beaten old pine tree;

A lone boat drifts and gulls fly on, while willows droop over shade.

This good season will fleet by, and flowers blooming now will wilt;

Only the rocks will remain, bearing the trace of the times gone by.

I regret that I cannot stay here long, lingering near the spot of fame;

As I hasten to leave at sunset, my heart aches to bid farewell to it.

第十一回 登龍湖亭

泓渟春水午初喧

遊子登臨倦入門

半壁風霜松樹老

一帆沙鳥柳陰昏

良辰荏苒花將盡

舊蹟蒼茫石有痕

只恨名區難久住

夕陽催別斷人魂

Upon Ascending Yong-ho Bower Again

Leaning on the railing, a wayfarer plays a flute in the west wind;
Sentiments inspiring lines call for an overflowing cup of wine.
Over the thick reeds and the wide stream, wild geese fly up high;
Leaves dying the village in red make the mountain look colder.
Sitting on a rock, I wet a brush in ink to write the title of my lines;
In the pine wood I hang my hat on a tree knot to wash my hair.
Pitying myself for facing the deepening autumn with a pale face,
I force myself to embrace an armful of yellow chrysanthemums.

第十二回　復登龍湖亭

一笛西風客倚欄
詩愁剩得酒杯寬
蒼葭水闊雁初起
紅葉村深山更寒
石上題名斜點筆
松間濯髮倒懸冠
自憐憔悴當秋甚
強把黃花爛熳看

Composed at Yong-ho Bower

As I sit by the river to indulge in peaceful leisure,
Calm wind and bright sunbeam fill the noontide air.
Moss-laden old walls bear the trace of bygone days;
Petals wilting in rain prove the rapidity of time's flow.
Barley fields and villages stretch far, hiding in valleys;
Both on land and water people remain busy in spring.
Getting inebriated at a bower of fame is a rare privilege;
Do not regret that we can stay here only for a short while.

第十三回　龍湖亭書懷

清遊爲卜大江前
風日妍妍向午天
古壁蒼苔尋往迹
落花疎雨感流年
麥麻村闊分雙峽
樵牧春忙競小船
一醉名亭難更得
諸君莫惜少留連

Upon Moving from Yong-ho Bower to a Boat Afloat

To keep our promise, I head to the small bower on a fine day;
The stretch of scenery along the river calls us to drifting on it.
At noontide we move to a boat afloat to continue composing;
Watching the red petals of plantain falling, we indulge in poesy.

第十四回　自龍湖亭移吟舟峙店

良辰赴約小亭頭
一路江光送我遊
向午移吟舟上店
紅蕉花下亦風流

In Celebration of the Sixtieth Birthday of Hwang Sŏk-jŏn

The renowned scholar Hwang Hyŏn has a brother, Sŏk-jŏn,
To whom heaven granted the blessing of being pure and high-minded.
His vehement argument reveals his peerless knowledge of history,
His seething passion for justice, and his undaunted spirit.
Friends and guests fill his house invigorated by gusto and zeal,
And words of wisdom and humor follow each overflowing cup.
He need not leave home to befriend scholars of fame,
For letters from afar keep arriving day and night.
Writings of petty poetic skills he has never cared for;
His first concern is to be a man and to do a man's work.
Poverty and illness have always followed him since childhood;
Nonetheless, he has never minded meals crude and coarse.

    It was in the cloud-encircled neighborhood that we were born
In the same year, though I was born a few months later.
For ten years in a room hardly protected from wind and rain,
We shared the same desk, reading together till dawn broke.

    Now in these turbulent times, a gift does not receive light,
And in this hopeless age we are men deprived of our nation.
There was a time when he roamed like a madman with unkempt hair,
Calling himself a vagrant dweller, whose abode is nature itself.
To have his revered brother's writings published in a volume,
He traveled far and wide to where they might be found and retrieved.
Having finally finished the work no one else could ever have done,
He alone could fully savor the joy, and cried in secret.

    Now his sixtieth birthday has come in the fair month of May,
The pomegranate petals are shed and the cherry blossoms are red.
Though his beloved wife is no longer around to see this happy day,

壽黃石田六十一初度

梅翁有弟號石田

傲慢清曠性出天

抵掌論史明千古

腔血輪囷氣翩翩

友客滿堂豪興發

雅謔紛紛落樽前

膽大坐交天下士

尺素日夜飛千里

小藝詩文亦不屑

男兒事業最許己

自少坎坷奈貧病

齷齪淡泊而已矣

憶曾共結白雲隣

同庚我是雌甲辰

十年風雨苟安室

併榻研粲無夕晨

粵自世革故潛光

待月軒中作遺民

有時被髮恣倡狂

自謂江湖一旅人

隻手拮据梅泉集

漢北淮南無不及

千金剞劂能事畢

獨自懽娛獨自泣

Their offspring have grown to be men of promises.

His nephews and cousins are all good at composing lines;

They in turn recite verses to wish him a long prosperous life.

The ancient art of medicine lately enchanted him,

And his knowledge and insight deepen as years pass.

With his long white beard and twinkling eyes,

He teaches us that a life of purity and modesty leads to longevity.

    I wished to attend the congratulatory feast,

But the stream swollen with rain barred me from being there.

As I have missed the chance to play the flute to a dancing crane,

I look toward the eastern hill, and only send my good wishes.

舊甲重回夏月中

榴花初落櫻桃紅

中堂琴瑟惜未諧

寶樹雙株藹春風

阿咸昆季摠能詩

迭唱新篇祝無窮

舊訣青囊晚更好

老去能知修鍊道

蒼鬐如戟眼如星

始信清羸證壽考

我欲隨人當賀席

適雨川漲未能渡

一笛未和鶴南飛

東望方壺空自禱

Composed in Relay at Yong-ho Bower

Muddy streams flow down, swirling and tumbling;
In dreary rainfall, rainbows fade and shoot up again. [My couplet]

[After returning to Ok-chŏn Inn at sunset]

Having remained a mountain wanderer for a while,
I have returned here to seek the spring river again.
Though the woodland path is dark, I am in no fear,
For the crescent moon befriends one heading home. [My quatrain]

第十五回　龍湖亭拈庚韻抽葉聯句

濁潦飜洄潏
霖霓乍晷盈　白村

[暮歸玉川店]

偶作山中客
更尋江上春
不愁林路黑
初月伴歸人　白村

Hummed Extempore in the Mountain

Acorn trees and chestnut trees densely stand alongside a stream;
Autumn sunlight falls warm, and casts dim shadows at midday.
Mountain birds must know what a man living in retreat wishes;
Each time turning toward my window, they sing whole-heartedly.

山中即事

橡栗扶疏挾一溪
秋陽暄曬午陰低
山禽似識幽人意
每向窗前款款啼

Upon Alternating Verses with Yi Sang-mu (1)

Shooting stars flash, falling into the wood;

    Fireflies glimmer blue, fleeting over the field.

Watermills divide the sound of water flowing;

    Lamplight escapes the wall of the dense trees.

As night deepens, sudden rainfall becomes louder;

    Through the dark bamboos a lone lamp glimmers.

My long sojourn here is due to the autumn rain,

    Yet noble personality is looked up to like clouds.

A moth's flutter may sweep off a weak candle flame,

    And a frog's faint croak may cause a branch to fall.

The remaining spring fades away with the sound of rain;

    The barking of a lonesome hound fades among clouds.

Chestnut burrs open up by themselves in the wind;

    Plantain leaves often lean, laden with dew.

The crescent moon looms only to fade away soon;

    Moonbeams that gradually lean fall on the lone pine.

Faint smoke arises from a worn cottage's roof;

    The declining moon throws light on green moss.

Gourds lie white on the fence made up of vines;

    Crystal clear dewdrops dangle on the thin cobwebs.

The shadow of the bamboos shatters moonlight;

    Grass and trees clear the smoke for heating cauldron.

Grass insects announce the coming of cold season;

    Fire set on the field looks as if it were dozing.

Wind turns a round leaf over to show its back;

    Flowers blossoming high are adjoined with dew.

In the quiet mountain the sound of beating cloth echoes;

與李相武共吟(其一)

流星穿樹白

暗燐走郊青

野碓橫分澗

山燈迥出林

夜深聽急雨

竹暗見孤燈

客久偏秋雨

人高可贈雲

細蝶吹殘燭

輕蛙墮綠枝

殘春鳴雨外

孤犬響雲間

栗房風自坼

蕉葉露頻傾

初月生旋落

孤松光漸斜

孤烟生白屋

落月照蒼苔

匏子跨籬白

蛛絲胃露明

竹陰紛碎月

草樹淡蒸烟

林虫寒自語

野火迥如眠

Under a quiet lamp a lone cricket keeps chirping.
All mountains are there for people to climb;

   Flowers shed their petals for those bidding farewell.
As the mountains are near, they look like canopies;

   As the stream is clear, it shines like a frost beam.
Frosty season draws near to hasten leaves turning red;

   Autumn sunrays are warm on belatedly ripening rice field.
Children go to wood to collect cracking chestnut burrs;

   A bird skips off water, holding a snatched fish in its beak.
When dusk comes, a country cow returns to her stable by herself;

   When night comes, birds return to their nests under the eaves.
In the bright lamplight, flies turn even more vigorous;

   Under the hollow eaves, a spider leisurely crawls on its web.
On both sides of the bank, rice turns yellow, while ripening;

   In the lone village, trees turn colorful, wearing autumn leaves.
Early frost melts away the moment it falls on the ground;

   Mist and fog hide densely grown trees of their own accord.
In a region of moral distinction, no vulgar practice is found,

   And one meets a man of noble nature in a remote village.
A water-bird becomes startled to see the moon setting over the hill;

   The hill resounds with the echo of pounding the crops at night.
The cicadas chirping at the eaves are noisy in the burning sun;

   Small ants on the yard slowly crawl to their sand holes.
When fruits get ripened, frost starts falling abundantly;

   As leaves turn dry, wind blows lightly, though uninvited.
Rivulets in autumn murmur to the bamboo-framed window;

   The cold moon looms to float over the brushwood gate.
As paulownia withers, wind rushes its leaves to fall;

   As bamboos grow green, rain presses down their stalks.

圓葉風飜背
高花露連頭
山虛雙杵應
燈靜一虫多
山多爲客地
花落送人時
山近疑重幕
川明似霜暉
霜近新楓早
秋暄晚稻香
童收黃栗去
鳥啄白魚飛
巷牛昏自入
簷鳥夜相還
燈明蠅猶健
簷虛蟢自流
兩岸稻禾熟
一村楓樹明
早霜難着地
深樹自籠烟
特地無淺俗
深村見好人
水禽驚落月
夜碓響青山
簷蟬烘日亂

Far on the distant field, clouds seem to crawl on the earth;

Over the empty pond, moonbeams float on its wave.

Pathos of an old man deepens in the autumn night;

Dream of a wayfarer makes a night much too long.

庭蟻遲沙行

果熟霜初重

葉乾風自輕

秋泉鳴竹戶

寒月上柴關

蕉老風摧葉

筠清雨壓梢

野迥雲粘地

潭虛月漾波

老愁秋更苦

旅夢夜偏長

Upon Alternating Verses with Yi Sang-mu (II)

A lamp brightens the quiet night in the autumn mountain, while
Over the cold village covered with red leaves, snowflakes flutter.
I awake upon hearing the downpour of rain ringing in the wood;
As I finish composing a poem, the Milky Way leans to the eaves.
Old people living in secluded villages still keep their old custom;
But youngsters who attend new schools keep uttering gibberish.
Over frost-laden chrysanthemums, a thin web is drawn entangled;
In the bright moonbeam, a nest of the swallows is seen aslant.

與李相武共吟 〔其二〕

青燈夜靜秋山宿
紅葉村寒早雪飛
睡起林間鳴驟雨
詩成簷外倒明河
耆老深村猶舊俗
兒童新校盡殊音
霜華細綴蜘蛛網
月彩斜窺燕子窠

Overjoyed over Chang I-pa's Visit (I)

Fleeting time has already brought the freezing winter;
And thick clouds press on scattered rocks and steep cliffs.
As my friend has crossed a mountain, as if it were a low hill,
New moon rises to float above trees, renewing her dear look.
Under a glimmering lamp, we cherish each moment of chatting,
While we, gray-haired, regret that we are to bid farewell soon.
I have heard apricot blossoms announce the coming of spring;
Lifting wine cups, we promise we shall get together again soon.

喜張二坡見訪 (其一)

年光荏苒到窮陰
亂石層崖雲正深
惟有故人踰短嶺
更憐新月出疎林
青灯似惜逍遙興
白首偏長送別心
聞道梅花春信早
共君杯酌約相尋

Overjoyed over Chang I-pa's Visit (II)

My friend frequently visits this poor village to see me;
How often has he trodden the path covered with new moss?
Having sent geese away to the far-off sky on a moonlit night,
I wait for apricots to bloom in the snow to bring news of spring.
Time flies, leaving not many evenings for indulging in wine;
Cockcrow at dawn makes me realize I still have much to read.
Now I've heard that an impending war is on its way, I fear
Many poor innocent people will soon wet kerchiefs with tears.
A leisurely man can see the clouds rising above the mountain;
Only when night deepens can one hear the watermill turning.
When bad harvest comes, people worry about the impending tax;
Autumn in drought is the right season for sowing barley seeds.
Faintly heard cockcrow tells that the village is still far away;
As the flickering lamplight dies out, only dreary night remains.
Yellow chrysanthemums renew their bright color in the rain;
Red leaves rustle of their own accord, though no wind blows.
Mountain path crawls on the steep slope to cross the rocky hill;
Tender palm leaves come adrift on the water flowing in the vale.
Dried-up bamboos are hewn from the dense wood of the garden;
The meandering lanes change their routes from time to time.
Trees bearing red leaves hide the path to take on the way to a tavern;
White clouds hide the turret for reading, burying it in haziness.
Dreams lead one to relive the dreary moments already in the past;
Happy poetic lines occasionally strike a man's brain unawares.
As the wind over the stream stops blowing, it feels even chillier;
When a rainy spell stops for a while, don't say it has cleared up.
Far-off trees finally bear yellow leaves drifting in the moonlight,

喜張二坡見訪（其二）

有友窮山訪我頻

幾回筇屐破苔新

天涯雁送三更月

雪裡梅傳舊國春

歲色無多沽酒夕

雞聲如促讀書人

忽聞海外干戈急

也洗蒼生淚滿巾

人閒正看山雲起

夜深猶聞澗碓靜

年荒預恤催粗日

秋旱偏宜下麥時

裊裊雞鳴村更遠

寥寥燈落夜偏長

黃花着雨還增色

赤葉無風自作聲

路懸斜穿岩崖出

楨細遙分澗水來

園篁每乾稠中伐

田路旋從捷處移

紅樹連藏沽酒路

白雲深掩讀書樓

夢因往事支離滓

詩或無心穩藉成

And the lone village lies tranquil, covered by a long stretch of fog.

As the mountain looms near, pines and vines lead to the village;

Deep into night, despite windy rain, lamplight is bright for the guest.

溪風乍定猶錄冷

霖日纔開莫謂晴

遠樹初黃飛細月

孤村一碧臥長烟

山近松蘿村逕晴

夜深風雨客燈明

At a Gathering at Pan-song Bower

While our cool garments reflect cold beams,
The crescent moon comes out of the wood.
On both slopes, the shadow of the trees moves;
Onto the stream, flowers cast their reflections.
Guests walk, listening to the sound of water;
The old monk keeps his mind serene as clouds.
I awake from a dream, as mounts begin to loom,
When I hear a gong resound and wind-bells ring.

第五回 芝川里盤松亭雅會

爽然衣帶冷

初月出空林

兩岸樹陰轉

一蹊花影深

客來流水響

僧老白雲心

夢驚山欲曉

鐘磬發清音

At the Eighteenth Gathering at Yong-ho Bower

We arrive at our dear spot when spring is about to fade;
Tall zelkovas and drooping willows fill the riverbanks.
Guests in love with green mountains ascend the bower;
The sunset glow urges those who cross the river to hurry.
As we take our seats on the soft grass spread on the bank,
Wind carries the pine scent to make us lift wine-cups often.
Inclination to return drifts away, as if borne on the boat;
And on the long stretch of sand falls rain thin like threads.

第十八回　龍湖亭雅集

一到名區已暮春

綠槐垂柳滿江新

青山若戀登樓客

落日偏催渡水人

兩岸莎平分座穩

半簾松冷擧杯頻

歸心忽與征帆轉

十里沙洲雨似塵

Spending a Night at Yong-du School

Through the pinewood by the river runs a lane, meandering;
Wearing bamboo-hats and straw-shoes, we walk in moonlight.
Fog that hides willow trees lingers where the ferry is moored;
Thin rain on peach blossoms makes the village look lonesome.
Children learning old teachings help to retain good old custom;
New ways of life becoming pervasive now only lead to worries.
A thatched hut with bamboos behind gives comfort to an onlooker;
The lanes winding through the field lead to the deep-seated yard.

同夜宿龍頭書塾

一江松翠逕微昏
笠屐紛紛帶月痕
楊柳疎烟迷古渡
桃花細雨暗孤村
兒童舊學猶敦俗
世路新風空斷魂
竹裏茅茨幽賞好
縱橫阡陌接深園

While Drinking at Yong-ho Bower

Dewdrops rolling down on reeds tell it is high autumn;
The river glittering with green light looks as if not flowing.
On a small ferry, fishermen and woodcutters argue about distance;
In the stream near shore, gulls and ducks plunge and come afloat again.
Green mountains offer the best places for our getting together;
Wearing white hair, we won't have many more days like this.
As we untie the boat to leave the autumn-tinted scene behind,
A song spreading over the waves moves the listeners to pathos.

第十九回　置酒龍湖亭

涓涓蒹露已高秋

淨綠江光滾不流

舟小漁樵爭遠近

渚清鷗鴨對沈浮

青山最好相逢地

白首無多此日遊

解纜楓根欲歸去

滄浪一曲動人愁

Drinking at Noontide at a Bower by a Stream

I climb the steep stairs, holding onto the gyrating railings;
On the bower built over a bridge, another floor soars higher.
The sound of the warbling stream floats over the green trees;
The entangled vines of wisteria crawl on the precipitous rock.
As the summer sky may soon be filled with frost and snow,
The field-loiterer's mind and soul become clearer than ever.
While praising beautiful scenery upon visiting an old temple,
I fear I try to cover eye-dazzling silk wear with a coarse coat.

溪樓午酌

危梯曲檻試初登
橋上飛樓更一層
淅瀝溪聲浮碧樹
嶄巖壁勢覆蒼藤
夏天冰雪如將逼
野客神魂倍覺澄
古寺若論形勝美
錦衣燦燦一裘增

Leaving a Mountain Path Behind

Wearing a bamboo-hat and straw-shoes, I walk through a wood;
Having come out to a wide-open field, I instantly miss the woodland.
I walk through the busy town to arrive at a shabby tavern by sunset;
Sitting on a chair in the shade of bamboos, I indulge in brief leisure.

出山口呼

笠屐聯翩亂樹間
出郊還復戀青山
放光村外斜陽店
竹裏胡床暫借閒

Drinking at Yong-ho Bower

I seek the nearby bower to receive some comfort;
Though raised tall, the lone bower has no gate.
Willows bearing the river's light stand far and near;
Peaches bloom in the wind neither warm nor cold.
Having walked on the open field and the flowery path,
I empty a bowl brimful of wine in the spring wind.
The day when I planted the pine was a short time ago;
I already see a big shadow it casts in the midday sun.

第二十回　赴飲龍湖亭

龍湖咫尺訪靈源
臺上孤亭不設門
楊柳江光無遠近
桃花天氣半寒暄
經來野驛芳菲路
倒盡春風灩瀲樽
手植庭松如昨日
團團已見午陰昏

At a Gathering in Ae-chŏn Dale

Pine roots and old rocks keep the torrent as their pillow;
Leisurely clouds spread wide don't drift away till noon.
If you ask a passerby to depict the scene in a few lines,
He'll babble on, telling how the stream started flowing.

第七回　會于艾川洞口

松根老石枕溪流
滿地閒雲午不收
若使遊人題勝境
百年應說此源頭

Staying Overnight at Yŏng-san Hall

To keep our promise to explore the famed mountain together,
We climb along the emerald cliffs and the flowery streams.
The path winds into a wood of tall pines and entangled vines;
Our dream lingers around the cloudy moon and many a peak.
If one wishes to shake off the worldly dust while living this life,
He'd better decide to live here in leisure till his hair turns white.
The songs of the orioles warbling in the wood renew my joy;
While walking with a staff and a jar of wine, I forget to return.

夜宿靈山殿

良辰結客訪名山
翠壁紅泉次第攀
路入松蘿千尺裏
夢懸雲月亂峰間
此生願謝紅塵累
特地將期白首閒
繞樹鶯聲情更款
一筇携酒不知還

Composing and Drinking at Yong-ho Bower

We've joyfully gotten together at this famed bower;

The narrow lane through pines remains befogged till noon.

As a windblown sailboat drifts, willows draw green branches;

In a lone village, wild flowers bloom boisterously after rain.

As spring comes, desire to ascend the bower becomes irresistible;

As one grows older, suppressing sentiments becomes even harder.

How often can we enjoy a gathering like this during our lifetime?

Don't hesitate to recite a poem loudly in front of a bowl of wine.

第二十二回　龍湖亭唱酬

名山結社喜相尋

挾路松雲轉午陰

遠棹迎風江柳綠

孤村經雨野花深

春來易發登臨興

老去偏多感慨心

此會百年能幾日

樽前莫惜一高吟

Staying Overnight at Hwa-ŏm Temple

As the dreary rain keeps me from climbing the green hill,
I hum lines all day long with the brushwood gate closed.
Over the wilting flowers, butterflies flutter as if in madness;
Above dense wood, leisurely clouds linger, reluctant to fly off.
Having contemplated composing lines worthy of Su Tung-Po,
I ended up pawning my jacket at a shabby tavern—after Tu Fu.
A grand temple soaring high is worth trying to climb to visit;
Don't even mention turning our way back, leaning on staffs.

擬上鍾石臺　滯雨宿華嚴寺

苦雨無緣上翠微

沈吟終日掩松扉

花殘老蝶狂猶舞

樹密閒雲濕不飛

佳節擬成蘇子賦

荒墟復典杜翁衣

琳宮百尺登臨好

莫道遊筇遽爾歸

Forced by Rain to Spend Two Nights at an Inn

Whirlwind has brought a downpour on a thousand peaks;
It is time for a wayfarer to wake up from his dream.
Sound of the gong fades, as the torrent howls louder;
Faint lamplight glimmers between densely arrayed trees.
Growing old, I resort to drinking more often than before;
Whenever I feel laden with sadness, I turn to reading.
Ardor for poetic composition drifts away with clouds;
What remains after much thinking is sheer emptiness.

芙蓉館滯雨信宿

冥颼千峰雨

羇人夢覺初

鍾聲隨澗轉

燈影出林疎

老去猶耽酒

愁來更看書

詩境雲俱遠

空寂入思餘

Dropping by a Village Tavern after Descending a Mountain

Putting on a coat and a bamboo-hat in haste, I headed to the bridge;
Fog spread in the wood was dampening the wind blowing at noon.
I complained last night, saying it had rained enough in the mountain;
But then the village was drowning in the sound of a heavy downpour.

出山抵西村店

紛紛衣笠出橋東
樹裏嵐光滴午風
剩說前宵山雨惡
人家泛在水聲中

At a Gathering at Ae-chŏn Vale

We've gathered in the vale to send off the spring receding;
Spring flowers are gone to allow green to replace them.
Humming lines all day long, we've become carefree loafers;
Sitting around the crock, we regret that we are to part soon.

第九回　會于艾泉洞

谷口相尋惜暮春
名花已老綠陰新
行吟盡日清狂客
摠是樽前恨別人

Staying Overnight at Pu-yong Inn

As the window begins to let in faint light at dawn,
I awake to hear an oriole singing in the west wood.
The sun turns bright to shine on the exuberant grass,
And the wood looks deep with the branches drooping.
Mountains remain the same as when they first arose;
As my hair turns white, I am awakened to my life's goal.
Urgent call for a poem sounds as loud as a temple gong;
As I hasten to finish, a wind-bell tinkles to tell it is noon.

宿芙蓉館

曉窓偏早起
鶯語在西林
茸茸晴暉上
離離綠樹深
青山猶太古
白首悟初心
激烈催詩鉢
還期午磬音

Upon Arriving at Yong-ho Bower with Wine

Unable to suppress the spring sentiments on a fine day,
We gathered at the bower with wine to breathe vernal air.
The rain-soaked bower wears green moss time has put on it;
Butterflies flutter over the flowers blooming near the brook.
The road to the station branches far over the exuberant grass;
The loiterers sit scattered in the shade of many a pine tree.
As we read new-composed lines of longing for a dreamland,
They sound more melodious than the tunes of a pipe or strings.

第二十五回　携酒至龍湖亭

麗日初晴興可憐

林亭携酒踏風烟

荒臺雨潤蒼苔合

絶澗花明白蝶懸

驛路迥分芳艸外

遊人散坐亂松前

新詩一唱江南曲

雅韻清凉勝管絃

On My Way to Chŏn-ŭn Temple

The crystal-clear stream winds and tumbles at every turn,
While it flows down in the shade of the exuberant pines.
From olden days, people have sought many a place of fame;
But now poets are gathered in a vale they have vied to visit.

第十回　泉隱道中

碧玉清流曲曲深
一蹊凉穿萬松陰
古今遊覽紛無數
爭及詩家此日尋

Staying Overnight at Sang-sŏn Temple

Eager to depict good scenery, I always carry ink and a brush;
To be relieved of many a thought, I lift the wine cup again.
Staying overnight at a temple keeps worldly thoughts far off;
You in the dusty world, why remain busy while growing old?

宿上禪庵

欲題佳境常携筆
爲遣幽懷更進觴
一宿靈源塵想遠
浮生何事老奔忙

Descending a Mountain

Precipitous slope brings back wariness; I descend
With my back stuck on rock after rock at every turn.
I cast my eyes on the hill where I lodged last night
To see the white clouds leisurely sailing far above it.

下山

路急心還竦
灣灣背石歸
回看經宿處
惟有白雲飛

Congratulating Chŏng Yŏng-ha on His Sixtieth Birthday

As your sixtieth birthday has arrived in the apricot-blossoming spring,
Your loving wife and filial offspring renew devotion and love for you.
Your sinews and vitality come from sustaining modest diet for life;
Your sight, physical and mental, enables you to compose and read poetry.
In old age, gratification comes from one's work being worthy of his gift;
At a feast for longevity, poetry frees people from the pressure of poverty.
We vie with one another in wishing you a life as prosperous as a pine;
How many joyful guests here, blowing flutes for a southbound crane!

壽丁杞軒永夏

孤辰正及臘梅春
寶瑟斑衣獻祝新
身健久經咬菜日
眼明能作解詩人
老年甘旨猶稱職
壽讌風流却忘貧
松柏岡陵爭祝賀
南飛鶴笛幾嘉賓

At a Poetic Gathering at Yong-ho Bower

That mountain is crowded with fragrant pines and green willows;
Can we bear watching petals drift in the air to follow the stream?
Spring receding from a scenic spot spurs poetic sentiments;
In the cool wind blowing on the lofty bower, wine proves its effect.
From the dense wood, a bird flies up to the wide-open sky;
On the wide river, a lone boat drifts, tossing on the wave.
Eager to return home, the boatman sings a song in full throat,
While the bamboo-fence along the river dyes his clothes in green.

龍湖亭雅會

松香柳綠滿山扉
忍見殘花逐水飛
勝地春闌詩思旺
高亭風冷醉痕微
林深一鳥戎戎出
江闊孤舟滾滾歸
欲向汀洲歌採採
苙籬翠色染人衣

At a Gathering at Hwa-ŏm Temple

Over the lane cold air spreads, while it looks like rain;

When the sun is about to set, we finally arrive at the stone gate.

Amid flowers flows a brook, making the monk's kitchen cool;

In the clouds, Buddha is seated deep in the beam of a lone lantern.

Though not much wine is ready to be served at tonight's meeting,

We, with white hair, still retain youthful ardor in our hearts.

Thanks to the blessing of being born contemporaneously,

We enjoy reciting our lines whenever we get together here.

第十一回　會于華嚴寺

磴道微寒雨色侵

石門斜日晚相尋

花間細瀑僧廚冷

雲裏孤燈佛座深

綠酒無多今夜會

白頭猶有少年心

此生賴被桑緣重

每到名山一朗吟

On the Way Downhill

Watching the lovely trees that soar high to the clear sky,
I rest at every turn of the stream to delay my descent.
The most endearing spot is where my ears are entertained,
While spring wind blows, bringing along an oriole's song.

出山途中

膩濃瓊樹天新晴
隔磵休休故未行
最有關情砭耳處
好風娜縷送流鶯

Lines Composed Together at Chŏn-ŭn Temple

[3 lines are lost]

As the chimes stop ringing, dawn begins to break blue.
As dusk comes to let the vines gleam in the moonlight,
In the cold mountain, white-haired men gather like stars.
We befriend a man who pierces through Buddha's thoughts;
Till night deepens, we lean our ears to listen to his talk.

泉隱寺共賦

[三行毀失]
一磬初收曉色青
歲暮烏藤來似月
山寒白髮會如星
交情又有蓉公在
夜久玄譚喜可聽

At a Gathering at Yong-ho Bower

As drooping willows and green pines hide the lone bower,
Mountain light over the railings suddenly brightens my eyes.
Fallen flakes of willow leaves roll, as they follow my staff,
And flying petals come after me to pile up on the empty yard.
White-haired, we watch spring fading away this year again;
Drinking filtered wine, let us not sober up till the day is gone.
As we unmoor the boat to return to the estuary for leave-taking,
We can hardly bear the tune of a flute the boatman blows at sunset.

龍湖亭雅會

柳陰松翠掩孤亭
欄外山光眼忽青
落絮任顛隨短杖
飛花自逐聚空庭
白頭又遣今春暮
綠酒休令此日醒
欲放扁舟歸別浦
夕陽漁笛亦堪聽

Staying Overnight at Chŏn-ŭn Temple

When a thousand peaks are being dyed in the hue of the setting sun,
I borrow a straw-mat to sit on and watch mountains fading away.
The road I shall tread is deep and long, winding through the wood;
While meditation leads to serenity, white clouds sail leisurely above.
My old friend already on the decline suffers from a long ailment;
It can be chilly in early summer, and thin clothes aren't good enough.
When this night is over, we may not so easily get together again;
You, cuckoo-birds singing amid the trees, don't rush us to bid farewell.

第十二回　宿泉隱寺

千峰秀色染斜暉
借着蒲團坐翠微
客路深長芳樹合
禪心寂寞白雲飛
故人已老憐沈痼
初夏猶凉厭薄衣
一宿桑緣難更得
林間杜宇莫催歸

Lines Hummed on the Way to Hwa-gae

I walk upstream—finally to be amidst many a mountain;
I find the road for fishermen and woodcutters runs endlessly.
When I finally arrive at Shin-hŭng Village, it is already noon;
Orioles sing to send the scent of flowers borne on the wind.

花開途中口號

一溪遡入萬山中
洞裏漁樵路不窮
行到新興逢日午
黃鸝啼送棟花風

At "Ear-Washing Rock" of Shin-hŭng Temple

Ten thousand peaks loom above the "Ear-Washing Rock";
Clear brooks flow on, and the shade of dense trees is thick.
I cast my eyes over a rock to see a patch of cloud rising;
I wonder if I have seen the portrait of "Master Lone Cloud."[1]

新興洗耳巖

洗耳巖頭萬疊峰
澗流清澈樹陰濃
忽看石上片雲起
畫出先生三昧容

---

[1] "Master Lone Cloud" is a literal translation of 'Ko-un' ('孤雲'), the pen name of Choe Chi-won (崔致遠, 857–?), who was a man of literary distinction of Shilla Dynasty. After spending several years as a high-ranking government official, both in China and Shilla, he became a recluse, and died in obscurity at his mountain abode. There is a legend about his demise: He is known to have become a *shinsŏn* (神仙), an unearthly being, neither human nor divine.

Staying Overnight at Son Jae-ryun's Home

Soaring high to the sky almost within its reach,
It hardly remains free from clouds and rain.
Rocks piled around it threaten to crumble anytime;
Entangled vines flow down of their own accord.
Sky looks low, as if one could reach the North Pole;
Heaven looks near enough for one to peep into Elysium.
Royal azaleas are still in bloom, as spring is not gone yet;
One can learn that change of season may not be punctual.

細石平田　宿孫在倫家

逼空成突兀
雲雨少晴時
累石危如墜
疎藤倒自垂
天低捫極宿
仙近夢靈芝
躑躅春猶在
知應氣序遲

At the Hermits' Hill

Now the hermits are gone, only the hill remains—
With the rocks wearing the moss time has daubed.
I humbly beseech you, spirits of the mountain!
Don't scold a world-weary loafer for loitering here.

集仙臺

仙歸但有坮
石老莓苔白
寄語告山靈
莫嗔浮世客

At the Gate to the Sky

A rock soaring high to the sky for countless eons
One day got cracked on the cliff to open up a gate.
As the footpath ends, I crawl on a slope to reach it;
As I pass through the narrow gate, the sky stretches far.

通天門

千古穹窿石
緣崖裂作門
路窮乘棧入
一竅破天昏

Heaven's King Peak[1]

Heaven has granted me fine weather for my excursion.
As I sit high on the peak, worldly ties seem trivial.
From a cave at immeasurable height, chilly wind blows;
And a sea of cloud and fog spreads, unbounded and serene.
Though sumptuously spent on creation, cosmic energy persists.
Climbing a slope like a turtle's back, I've shed off worldly dust.
The column supporting the sky tells me Elysium is not far off;
The ruler of the heavens may startle to hear a mortal's cough.

天王峰

天爲吾行假日晴
上峰高坐世緣輕
千尋窟宅罡風厲
萬里雲烟海水明
閱盡鴻濛凝淑氣
泛來鰲背脫塵情
撐空一柱三清近
帝座應驚咳唾聲

---

[1] "Heaven's King Peak" is a literal translation of '天王峰,' the highest peak of Chiri Mountains (智異山).

On My Way out of the Ravine

Barley has not turned brown, and the rice field is still green.
Whenever I arrive at a spot of good scenery, I stop walking.
A wayfarer, who enjoyed a grand view on the peak yesterday,
Stops at a tavern, where he lodged the other night on his way.

出峽途中

麥穗未黃秋葉青
每逢佳處去還停
上峰昨日尋眞客
又復雙磎綠樹亭

At the Temple of Twin Streams

(Visiting the Reverend Hŏ Jŏng-hae)

Jade-like streams flow down through densely arrayed trees;

The cool air surrounding the stone gate befits an autumn night.

A flowery scent lingers around the pedestal in the dim candlelight;

Bamboos' shadow ascends the railings, while the moon floats above.

The wayfarer has walked on the rocky ridges of many a peak;

His tie with Buddha has led him to lodge in a temple room tonight.

As the immaculate monk wholeheartedly welcomes a visitor,

He offers a meal consisting of bamboo shoots and bracken sprouts.

雙磎寺

(訪許淨海上人)

綠樹淋漓碧玉流

石門涼氣似清秋

花香繞榻龕燈迥

竹影登欄曉月浮

客路已經千嶂石

禪緣更續十方樓

淨師又有勤迎意

筍蕨慇懃獎我遊

Visiting Sang-sŏn Temple

Above my staff, white clouds sail, blooming;
Under my straw shoes, rivulets flow, singing.
Slowly treading a thousand peaks dressed in green,
I didn't know the sunset glow was ahead of me.

第十三回　上上禪菴

筇頭灩灩白雲生
屐底淙淙溪水鳴
倦踏千峰蒼翠色
不知前路夕陽横

A Night at a Temple

The far-off temple is seated near the blue sky;
The sand-bar along the river stretches far and endless.
A wayfarer visits a temple near a cliff in the clouds;
The monk draws water from a well between rocks.
The mountain of early summer is deep with late flowers;
As the gong stops ringing, the lonely moon is hung aloft.
Having climbed high, I've become closer to the hermit,
And have forgotten that my hair has already turned white.

禪菴夜

縹緲禪菴近碧天
汀洲南豁野無邊
客來翠壁雲中寺
僧汲丹砂石竇泉
初夏山深花自晚
上房鐘落月孤懸
登臨一夜仙緣重
頓忘人間白髮年

Drinking Awhile

A flower blooming bright fills up the empty mountain,
While snowflakes flutter, casting shadows over the fence.
The traveler on the river, drenched in the rain overnight,
Arrives at the temple late, for you've detained him awhile.

三殿小酌

空山的歷一株花
雪影紛紛墻外斜
野雨隔宵江上客
晚來爲汝到禪家

While Descending a Mountain

Although I do not mind getting wet,
Morning dew keeps falling from dense trees.
A mortal, for sure, can't be an equal to a wizard:
After spending two nights in the mountain, I descend.

下山道中

不惜客衣沾
樹深朝露瀉
仙凡迥自殊
信宿還仍下

At a Gathering near a Stream by the Pines

When spring is gone, who will not miss green grass?
As I get inebriated, my boyish longing comes back.
As white stones in a stream help to open unearthly scenery,
What if I come here often, with a staff, wearing straw shoes?

第十四回　松川雅會

春去誰無芳草恨
酒酣還發少年心
清川白石開幽境
笻屨何辭日日尋

A Night at a Temple

On a moonlit night, I seek the semi-paradise, where
I forget my age of decrepitude under the dried-up vines.
Crossing lamplights beam through the falling petals;
The shadow of the pagoda reaches deep into the trees.
Having tasted all the pleasures of the dusty world,
I enjoy a peaceful sleep in the mountain I chance to enter.
I awake to realize that I am freed from all secular ties;
After burning incense deep in my soul, I bow to Buddha.

第十五回　靈山殿夜話

夜月行尋兜率天
枯藤忘却我衰年
燈光錯落花間出
塔影橫長樹裏連
浮世歡娛無隙地
名山邂逅借安眠
夢起六根清似洗
心香一爇拜龕前

At a Gathering at Yong-ho Bower

Having rushed to attend a gathering at this riverside village,
We are overjoyed to see one another before spring goes away.
Fragrant grass grows fast in the rain that blesses the season;
Remaining flowers are the cups we lift to wish friends well.
In the shade of flowers, our garments look refreshed at noon;
Thick moss covering rocks spreads the scent of time's flow.
While we indulge in the pleasure of singing and whistling,
We are unaware that the sun is about to set over the railing.

龍湖亭雅會

風騷一契動江鄉
春暮相尋興更長
芳草易成佳節雨
殘花爲送故人觴
芳陰午暖衣生潤
古篆苔深石有香
迭宕我歌君嘯樂
不知欄外已斜陽

Discussing Poetry with Sŏk-jŏng[1]

Though hills loom to block you, you've sought this village;
In this early spring, snowy wind has not yet completely gone.
In dim lamplight your old brush glides, bearing cloud and fog;
Though your body wanes, you still hear the crane in the wind.
My hut is shabby, but I am delighted that you stay overnight;
Grown old, you are glad to see a man smacking of some gift.
Deep into night, we don't feel tired of chatting and laughing,
Till we realize, all of a sudden, that the moon fades at dawn.

與石亭拈劉隨洲集得城字

海岳迢迢訪碧城
早春風雪未全晴
紅燈筆老雲霞氣
病枕天寒鸛鶴聲
貧屋正勤留客意
暮年猶切愛才情
夜深談笑還忘倦
已見龍岡曉月生

---

[1] Sŏk-jŏng (石亭) is the pen-name of Yi Chŏng-jik (李定稷, 1841–1910), a renowned scholar and poet, who also attained the zenith's height in calligraphy and landscape drawing.

Verses Dedicated to Master Sŏk-jŏng

Attending on you in the royal town[1] in bygone days,
I followed you on the rocky paths to the clear streams.
This has come to be known as a deed commendable,
And people in this county compete to recite your lines.

Once separated, I send you good wishes over the far-off sky,
While wild geese flock high slowly as the year recedes.
Clouds have stopped sailing, and even their flakes look azure,
As I wake up from daydreaming to look out of the window.

Not fearing the cold of the spring, I ventured on a wayfaring
To seek you, who dwell in a bush of knotgrass, over a brook.
I needed not ask a passerby how to find a way to your cot:
I recognized your cough heard from the shade of an apricot tree.

Though a hoary man and a young one had been exchanging letters,
Upon getting together at long last, we felt as if we were strangers.
But our mutual longing made us unaware of the brief spring night,
While we chatted in the dim lamp light till the moon faded at dawn.

Your poverty-ridden hut contains the six volumes of the Classical Canon;[2]
Even the darkest corner of your room is brightened by their presence.
Day in and day out, you remain busy correcting your old manuscripts,

---

[1] 'The royal town' is a direct translation of '鳳城' in the original poem. But actually it alludes to Kuryĕ (求禮), a county in Chŏlla Province, where the poet was born and lived.

[2] 'The six volumes of the Classical Canon' are: *The Book of Changes* (周易), *The Book of Poetry* (詩經), *The Scripture of Documents* (書經), *The Chronicles of Lu* (春秋), *The Book of Rites* (禮記), and *The Book of Music* (樂記).

呈石亭先生絕句八首

鳳城昔日共追隨
行盡山巖與水湄
此事至今傳美俗
郡人爭誦我師詩

一別天涯寄遠思
關河世暮雁來遲
停雲渺渺茳蘺綠
正是山窓夢罷時

不怕春寒尚遠行
蓼橋西北訪先生
逢人不問仙莊路
記取梅陰警咳聲

皓首青衿爛照書
戀餘相見若相疎
情深不省春宵短
坐到燈昏月落初

家貧猶有六經存
井火丹深絳帳昏
日向床翡刪舊稿
不嫌皓首臥孤村

正路蒼蒼末遍尋
千峰林壑鎖雲深

And embrace your life at a deserted village, while your hair turns white.

Though the right path is long and dreary, you have never swerved.
Though thick clouds block the road leading to the countless peaks,
Knowing that you can reach them, no matter how high, all alone,
You have never relinquished, though a wild beast confronted you.

Surrounded by velvety books piled up as if to embrace you,
You wield your wonted brush to reveal your overflowing thoughts.
As a light wind blows, bearing thin rain streaks hither and thither,
One may misconstrue it as the rustle of the bamboo leaves.

Above the paddies immersed brimful in water, white birds fly on,
And the morning sun rising throws beams on the wayfarer's wear.
Unable to suppress the rising sentiment over bidding farewell,
Many a branch of the willow wavers toward the visitor leaving.

懸知絕頂能孤往
虎豹當前不易心

縑素盈席縱復衛
幽情時逐老毫生
輕風颯颯吹練雨
認得閒窗幅竹聲

野水漫漫白鳥飛
碧城朝日上征衣
重楊似管離懷重
苦拂千絲向客歸

To Master Sŏk-jŏng

The village where knotgrass blooms lies near the sea;

The home of my old master Sŏk-jŏng[1] is in that village.

Living in a crumbling hut, he endures cold and hunger;

Relieving hunger with crumbs and chaff, he ignores the kettle.

Having read ten thousand books, he feels his stomach is full;

Strolling on straw sandals, he hums lofty lines that shatter rocks.

When he wields rhetoric, he traces back to the North Song period;

In expounding logic, he starts from the very beginning of learning.

In poetic composition, he extols Du Fu[2] as his supreme mentor;

In calligraphy, he wields his brush only to match Yan Zhenqing.[3]

His misty strokes lie somewhere between Mi Fu[4] and Huang Tingjian.[5]

Who will discuss the works of Zhishan[6] and Sŏk-jŏn[7] after him?

A worldly man cannot see things right, even with wide-open eyes;

Having settled in retreat, he is not aware of his beard turning white.

My hut is seated since olden days deep in a cloud-encircled mountain;

Rocks keep rolling down, so we have to stir the gravels with staffs.

Whenever we get together, he accepts me, a junior, as a pal of his;

Has there been another so humble to a younger one following his steps?

Chatting knee to knee, we are not aware that dawn is coming;

His jade-like uttering turns into powder to float in the air.

---

[1] Sŏk-jŏng (石亭) is the pen-name of Yi Chŏng-jik (李定稷, 1841–1910), a renowned scholar and poet, who also attained the zenith's height in calligraphy and landscape drawing.

[2] Du Fu (杜甫, 712–770) was a Chinese poet of the Tang (唐) dynasty. Along with his contemporary Li Bai (李白), he is frequently extolled as the greatest of the Chinese poets.

[3] Yan Zhenqing (顔眞卿, 709–785) was a nonpareil Chinese calligrapher of the Tang (唐) dynasty.

[4] Mi Fu (米芾, 1051–1107) was a Chinese painter, poet and calligrapher of the Song (宋) dynasty.

[5] Huang Tingjian (黃庭堅, 1045–1105) was a calligrapher, painter, and poet of the Song (宋) dynasty China.

[6] Zhishan (枝山) is the pen-name of Zhu Yunming (祝允明, 1460–1527), a scholar and calligrapher of the Ming (明) dynasty China.

[7] Sŏk-jŏn (石田) was the pen-name of Hwang Wŏn (黃瑗, 1870–?), younger brother of Hwang Hyŏn (黃玹, 1855–1910), the poet's mentor.

呈石亭先生

蓼花村落濱于海
石亭老人家此在
破屋天寒工忍飢
糅藜充然笑鼎鼐
萬卷根柢拄五內
曳履高歌金石碎
文章意度溯北宋
談說正始之初載
風騷我師老杜存
波礫晚屈顏平原
煙雲又在米黃間
枝山石田誰復論
世人瞠吹摠未知
一臥滄洲生白髭
我家昔在雲山深
喦花再落搖笭枝
見輒忘年嘆知己
前輩謙虛孰如此
迸談低膝夜易晨
珠唾玉屑紛然起
島瘦郊寒摠由天
萬事只付燒餘篇
聞道弧辰屬今歲
挹邱拍厓開觴筵

As the poems of Jia Dao[1] and Meng Jiao[2] end with sad notes,

His poems do end in sadness, encompassing all worldly affairs.

I am aware that his sixtieth birthday will come soon this year;

A banquet will be held on the slope of a hill exuberant with green.

Let the clear stream flow down, the way his remaining life will go on;

Let the endless spring breeze blow, spreading the vernal spirit wide.

As the starlight of the South Pole pours in to brighten his window,

Let the bright moonbeams flow in, bearing the ardor of a rolling wheel.

In the yard, his offspring will stand in array like exuberant trees;

And his pupils will compete to offer cups to wish his longevity.

His eyesight is still youthful enough for him to read small prints,

And his strong legs have enabled him to tour all the mounts of fame.

People talk about those who live gracefully with elevated poesy;

They need not look far, for he is an unearthly man treading the earth.

Driven to this nook where rainy wind blows, I send him my best wishes,

Though my lines, as in olden days, are like forcefully trimmed branches.

I regret I cannot now sit with him to learn how to choose the right words,

And no one is nearby, with whom to discuss how to improve my lines.

Though I have thought about reading these lines at a gathering,

I cannot think of one who may give me helpful suggestions.

I wish I could show these lines to a childhood friend of mine;

But we are far away from each other, though we long to be together.

I wish for him again that soft wind will blow on a pair of cranes,

And year after year, spring will be renewed, bringing much happiness.

---

[1] Jia Dao (贾岛, 779–843) was a Chinese Buddhist monk and poet of the Tang (唐) dynasty.
[2] Meng Jiao (孟郊, 751–814) was a Chinese poet during the Tang dynasty.

碧骨湖水清無涯

萬斛春風溢流霞

南極祥光爛射牖

微黃如月圓如車

庭前寶樹常若若

絳帳諸生幷侑酌

蠅頭細字眼如火

腳窮名山何矗鑠

風流雅韻世空比

地行仙人此真是

天涯風雨一瓣香

拙詩依舊磨驢技

恨未與署羅相比

無期無導論文字

爲向臺中探營誇

不辨評隣微有異

逢想詰人需幼隣

隔在江南相憶素

更願好風吹雙鶴

年年隨福來及春

Remembering a Friend at the Year's End

As heavy snow falls on the west hill, my hut looks even flatter;

My childhood friend is gone, leaving me in the chill of dawn.

I pray you, don't regret, saying you didn't live a life worthy of you.

When the time comes, a stallion will gallop apace in the howling wind.

歲暮懷人

雪壓西山老屋低

斑衣零落曉淒淒

請君莫說塩車苦

會見長風展驥蹄

About the Translator

Sung-Il Lee is the poet's grandson, born in 1943, the year of the poet's demise. He studied English literature at Yonsei University (B.A., 1967), University of California at Davis (M.A., 1973), and Texas Tech University (Ph.D., 1980). He is Professor Emeritus of Yonsei University, where he taught from 1981 till he retired in 2009. While he was on leave of absence, he taught as a visiting professor at University of Toronto (1987), University of Washington (1994–1995), and as a Fulbright Scholar-in-Residence at Troy University (2002–2003).

He has translated Korean poetry, both classical and modern, into English, and has published eleven anthologies: *The Wind and the Waves: Four Modern Korean Poets* (1989), *The Moonlit Pond: Korean Classical Poems in Chinese* (1998), which was on the list of the Outstanding Academic Books of 1998, selected by *Choice*, *The Brush and the Sword: Kasa, Korean Classical Poems in Prose* (2009), *Blue Stallion: Poems of Yu Chi-whan* (2011), *The Crane in the Clouds: Shijo, Korean Classical Poems in the Vernacular* (2013), *The Vertex: Poems of Yi Yook-sa* (2014), *Nostalgia: Poems of Chung Ji-yong* (2017), *Shedding of the Petals: Poems of Cho Jihoon* (2019), *Do You Know That Faraway Land? Poems of Shin Sŏk-jŏng* (2020), *Does Spring Come Also to These Ravished fields? Poems of Yi Sang-hwa* (2022), and *Counting the Stars at Night: The Complete Works in Verse and Prose by Yoon Dong-ju* (2022). For his English translation of Korean poetry into English, he received the Grand Prize in the Literary Awards of the Republic of Korea (1990) and the Korean Literature Translation Award (1999), both given by The Korean Culture and Arts Foundation. His Modern English verse translation of *Beowulf, Beowulf in Parallel Texts* (2017), is now at Bodleian Library.

Made in United States
Cleveland, OH
19 April 2025